I CAN COOK

Getting ready	2	Cookie faces	18
Jelly turtle	4	Pasta house	20
Mallow shapes	6	Toffee and date pud	22
Potato heads	8	Pizza snake	24
Rainbow slush	10	Popchoc treats	26
Giant cookie	12	Jam tarts	28
Monster cake	14	Magic marble cake	30
Surprise bread	16	Choc fudge icing	32

Author: J. Bastyra and C. Bradley

Illustrated by Michael Evans

Photography by Howard Allman

Series editor: Paula Borton

Series Designer: Robert Walster

© 1996 Watts Books

Watts Books
96 Leonard Street
London EC2A 4RH

Franklin Watts Australia
14 Mars Road
Lane Cove
NSW 2066

UK ISBN: 0 7496 2037 4
Dewey Decimal Classification: 641.5

A CIP catalogue record for this book is available from the British Library.

Printed in Malaysia

10 9 8 7 6 5 4 3 2 1

Getting ready

Before you start, read the recipe and look at the pictures to make sure you have all the ingredients and equipment you need.

Measure out the ingredients carefully. The oven needs at least 15 minutes to warm up, so don't forget to switch it on.

Be prepared

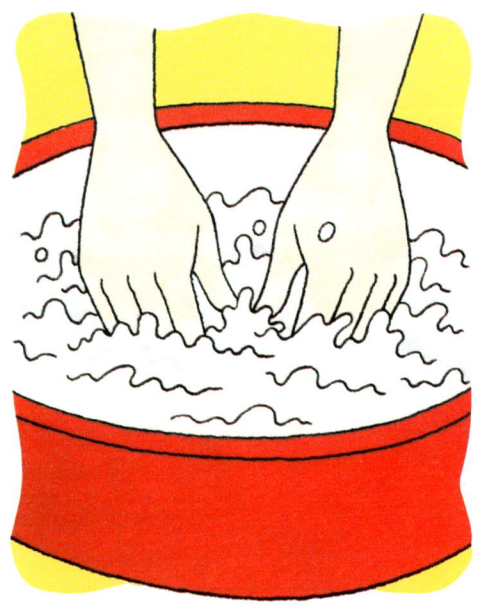

Don't forget to wash your hands before you start. Be careful with knives. If you have to use a sharp knife ask for help.

Remember to wear oven gloves if you are going to touch anything hot. Ask a grown-up to put dishes in or take them out of the oven for you.

Be especially careful when you cook anything on top of the stove. Remember to turn saucepan handles to one side.

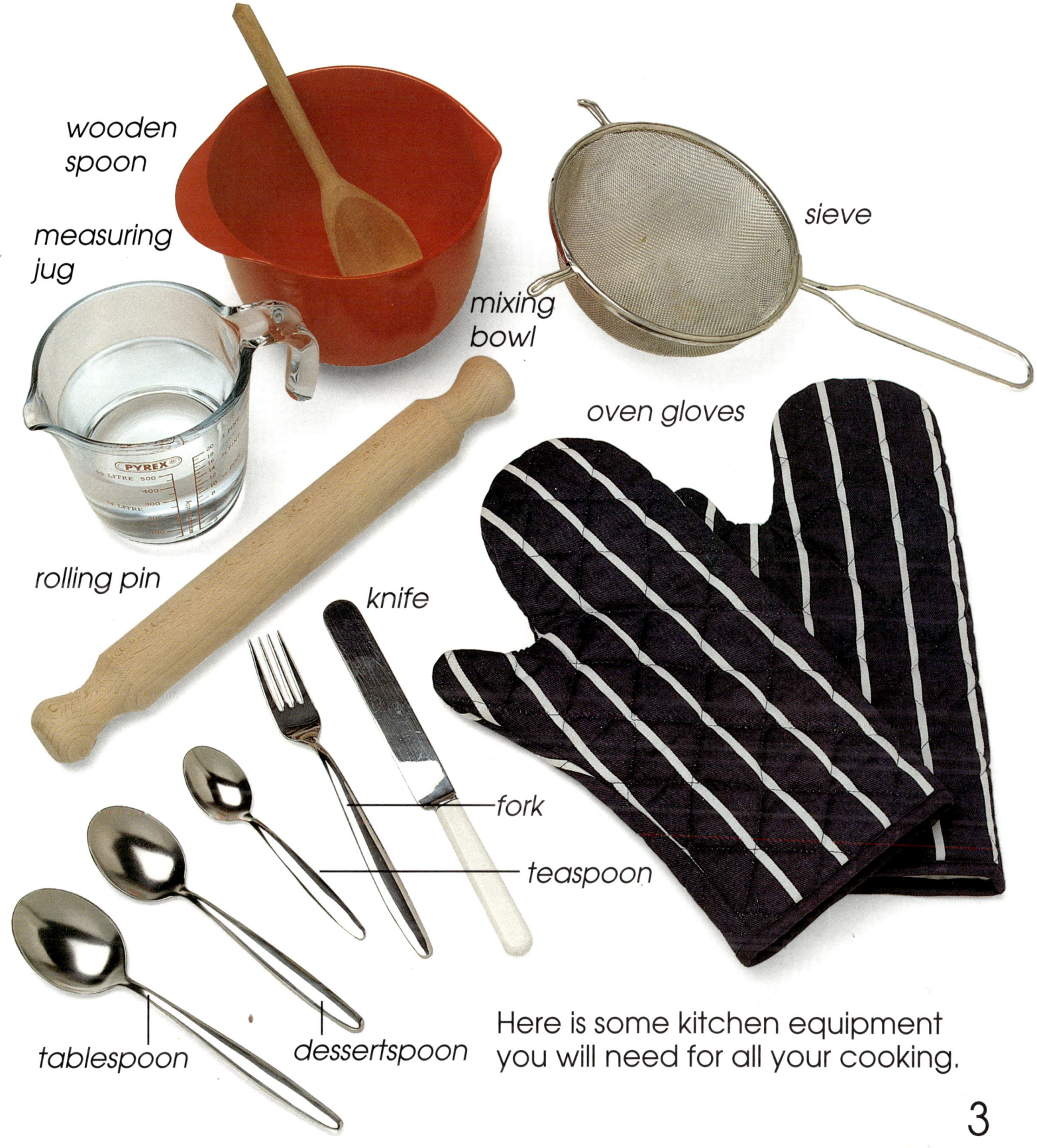

Here is some kitchen equipment you will need for all your cooking.

Jelly turtle

You will need:

- 1 packet of green jelly
- (600ml/1 pint) heatproof bowl
- black grape
- 2 kiwi fruit

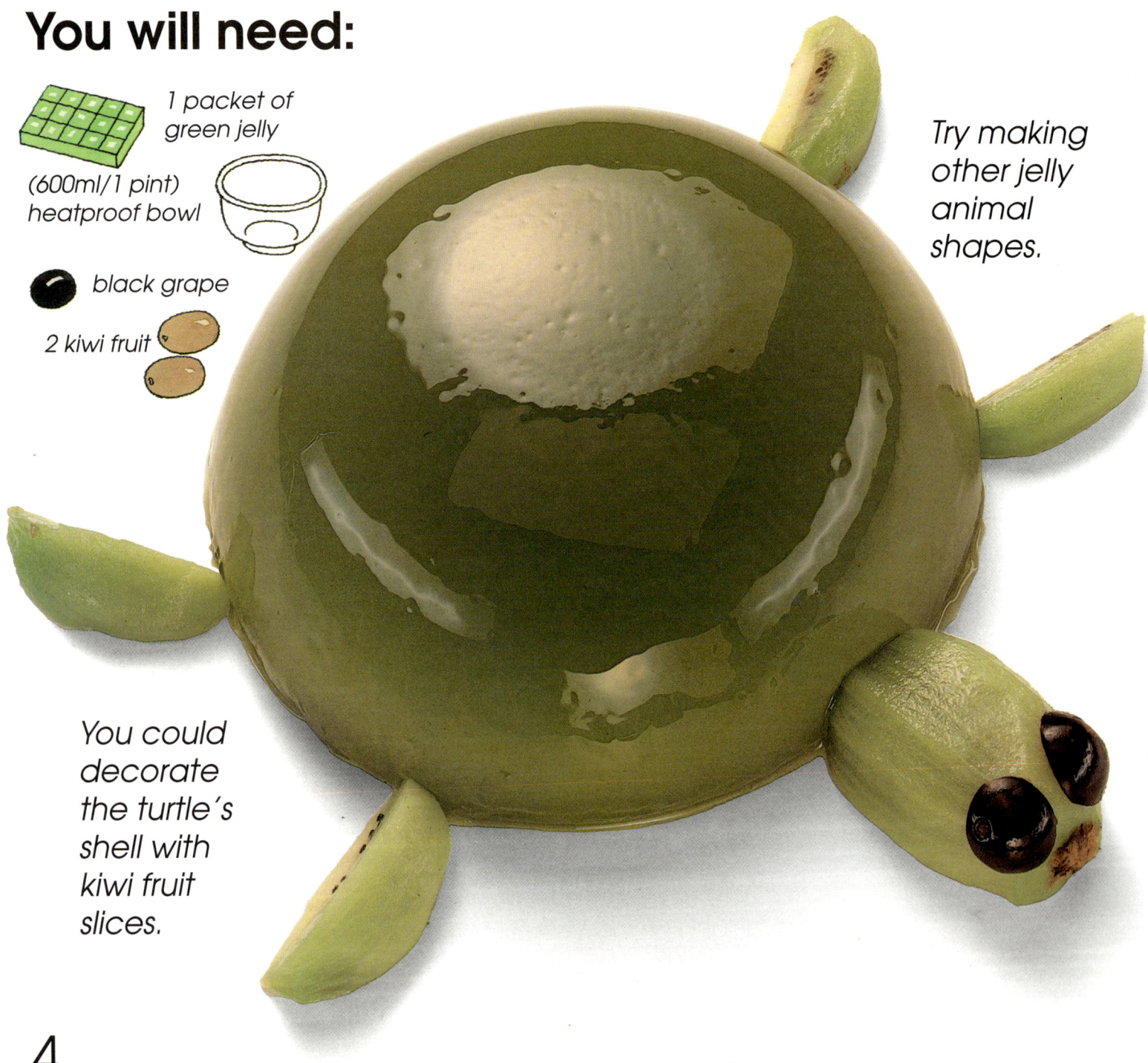

Try making other jelly animal shapes.

You could decorate the turtle's shell with kiwi fruit slices.

1.

Make the jelly following the directions on the packet. Put it in the fridge until set.

2.

Dip the bottom of the bowl into a basin of hot water and run a knife around the edge.

3.

Carefully turn out the jelly onto a big plate. Ask someone to help. Now peel the kiwi fruit.

4.

Use one kiwi for the head. Cut the other into four for legs. Use half a grape for each eye.

Mallow shapes

You will need:

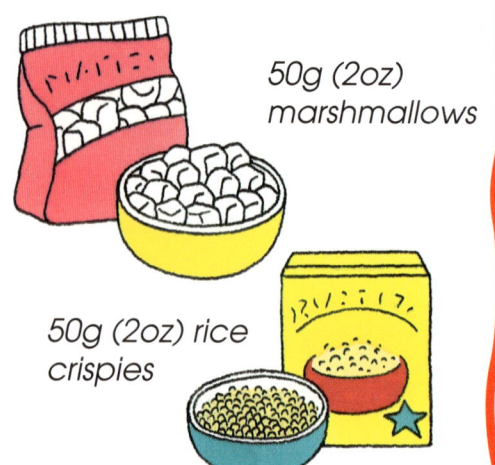

50g (2oz) marshmallows

50g (2oz) rice crispies

Before you start
Set your oven at 180°C/350°F/ gas mark 4. If you have a microwave put the marshmallows with the rice crispies in a covered bowl. Microwave for 1-2 minutes on medium.

1.

Mix the marshmallows and rice crispies in an ovenproof bowl. Put it in the oven for about 20 minutes.

2.

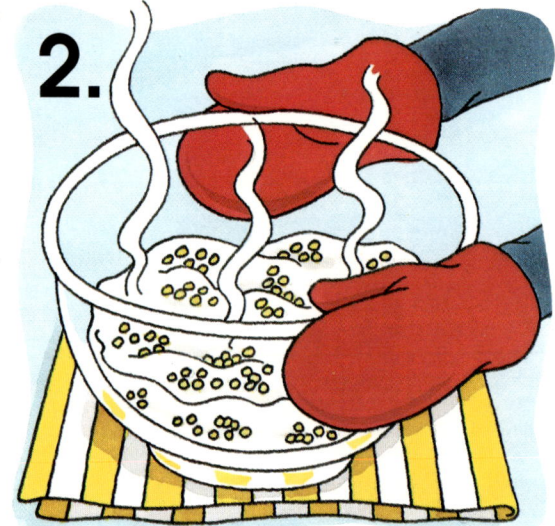

Take the bowl out of the oven and place it on a cloth.

Decorate your shapes with sweets.

You can make any shape you like. Try copying these ducks.

3. Mix the crispies and melted marshmallows with a wooden spoon.

4. Make shapes by pushing the mixture into moulds or form your own shapes. Do this before the mixture gets hard.

Potato heads

Before you start
Set your oven to 190°C/ 375°F/ gas mark 5.
If you have a microwave, wrap the potatoes in kitchen towel and cook on high for ten minutes

You will need:

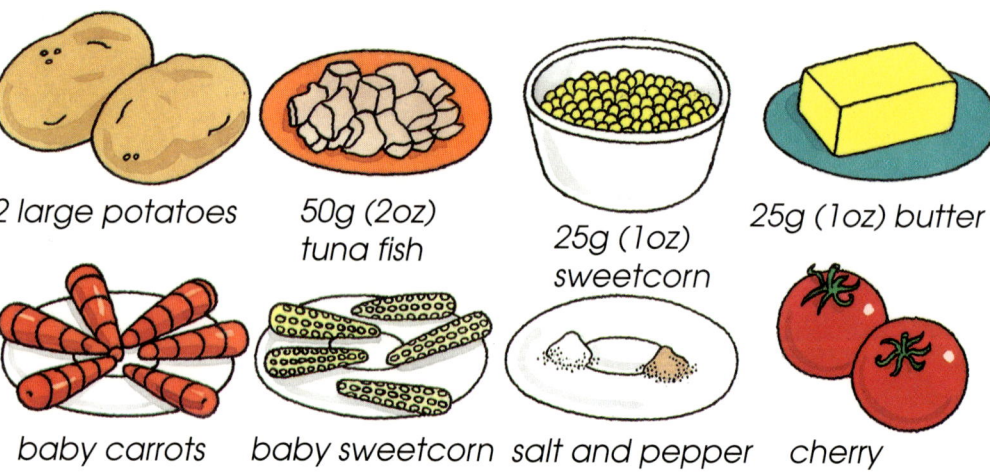

2 large potatoes 50g (2oz) tuna fish 25g (1oz) sweetcorn 25g (1oz) butter

baby carrots baby sweetcorn salt and pepper cherry tomatoes

1.

Scrub the potatoes and prick them with a fork. Bake them for 45 minutes.

2.

Cut the potatoes in half longways. Scoop out the soft insides into a bowl. Mix in the tuna, corn, butter and salt and pepper.

You can also use cucumber for ears, eyebrows and hair.

3.

Stuff the mixture back into the potato skins and smooth it with the back of a spoon.

4.

Put the potatoes on plates, and make faces, legs and arms with vegetables.

9

Rainbow slush

You will need:

orange juice

blackcurrant cordial

lime or strawberry cordial

ice cube trays

You can make your slushes any flavour or colour you like.

This slushy ice is delicious on a hot day. You can make these slushes any flavour you like.
 If you don't have any ice cube trays, use shallow plastic dishes.

1.

Pour the juices into three ice cube trays. One tray for each colour.

2.

Put the trays in the freezer for about 2-2½ hours.

3.

Take the trays out and drop the cubes from one tray into a jug. Mash the ice with a fork.

4.

Pour the slush into glasses. Do the same with the other two flavours to make three layers.

Giant cookie

You will need:

75g (3oz) margarine

75g (3oz) caster sugar

100g (4oz) self-raising flour

½ teaspoon vanilla essence

120ml (4fl oz) milk

50g (2oz) chocolate chips

2 teaspoons cocoa powder

Decorate with chocolate fudge icing (see page 32) and sweets.

Before you start
Set your oven to 180°C/350°F/gas mark 4.
Line a flan dish with foil.

1. Mix the margarine and sugar together in a bowl until light and fluffy.

2. Slowly stir in the flour, then add the chocolate. Use a wooden spoon to mix.

3. Mix in the vanilla essence, cocoa and milk.

4. Spread the mixture into the flan dish. Bake for 25 minutes.

Monster cake

You will need:

2 medium eggs

100g (4oz) margarine or butter

sweets

100g (4oz) self-raising flour

100g (4oz) caster sugar

butter cream icing (see page 19). Make some green and some yellow. Leave a little bit white.

1 teaspoon vanilla essence

paper petit fours cases

Arrange your cakes on a big tray or straight onto the table.

Before you start
Set your oven at 180°C/350°F/gas mark 4. Put the paper cases on a baking sheet.

1.

Mix the butter and sugar until it is all light and fluffy.

2.

Add the eggs and flour and beat it all until it is smooth. Add the vanilla.

3.

Drop teaspoons of mixture into the cases and bake for about 12 minutes. Cool on a wire rack.

4.

Ice the cakes yellow and green. Make one white. Arrange them as shown here. Add the sweets.

Surprise bread

You will need:

450g (1lb) plain flour plus a bit extra

1 sachet of easy blend yeast

360ml (12fl oz) hot water

1 teaspoon oil

100g (4oz) plain or milk chocolate

450g (1lb) loaf tin

1 teaspoon milk

Before you start
Oil the loaf tin to stop your bread sticking. Set your oven to 200°C/400°F/gas mark 6.

1.
Sift the flour into a bowl and sprinkle on the yeast.

2.
Mix in the hot water and oil to make a dough ball.

3.
Sprinkle flour onto a surface and knead the dough on it by pushing and pulling it with your hands.

4.
Put the dough in a clean bowl. Cover it and leave it to rise for an hour.

5.
Then put half the dough into the tin and scatter on the chocolate.

6.
Add the rest of the dough and brush the top with milk. Bake for 30-35 minutes.

Cookie faces

You will need:

Glacé icing
- 100g (4oz) icing sugar 
- 2 tablespoons water 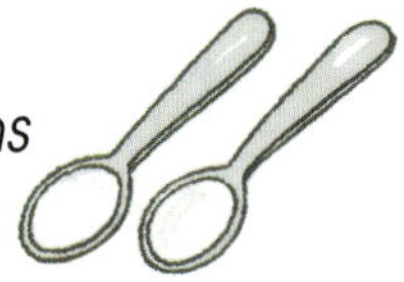
- food colouring* 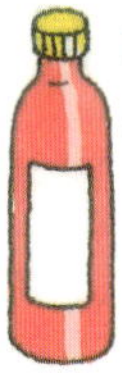
- plain biscuits 

Butter cream icing
- 50g (2oz) butter or margarine 
- 200g (8oz) icing sugar 
- 1 tablespoon milk 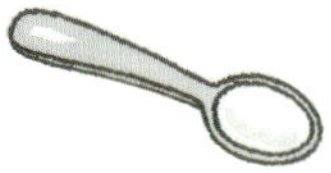
- sweets for decoration 

Make lots of funny faces.

Glacé icing

1. Sift the icing sugar into a bowl. Stir in the water.

2. To add colouring, mix in a few drops at a time.

Butter cream icing

1. Soften the butter by mixing it with a wooden spoon.

2. Sift in the icing sugar and then carefully stir it in.

3. Add the milk and stir in a colour or flavour (see the box below).

Decorating

1. Spread the icing on the biscuits. Dip your knife into water after every spread. This makes the job easier.

2. Leave the icing to set for a few minutes, then add the decorations.

> You can flavour or colour butter icing. Try adding lemon, cocoa powder or melted chocolate.

*You can buy natural food colours in health food stores.

Pasta house

Use celery sticks for trees.

Make your house on a foil-covered tray.

You will need:

200g (8oz) of pasta twists in three colours

celery

strips of cucumber for window frames

cherry tomatoes

cheese squares

60ml (2fl oz) olive oil

1 tablespoon wine vinegar

salt and pepper

1 teaspoon sugar

1.

Boil the pasta shapes in salted water for about 8 minutes. Ask someone to do this for you.

2.

Mix the sugar, salt, pepper and vinegar in a jug. Slowly add the olive oil, beating with a fork.

3.

Ask an adult to drain the pasta and put it in a bowl. Pour on the dressing and let the pasta cool.

4.

Make your house. Start with the frame and then fill in. Use cheese for the door and windows.

Toffee and date pud

You will need:

125g (5oz) sugared chopped dates - soak them in hot water for an hour

25g (1oz) butter

2 eggs

pinch of salt

200g (8oz) caster sugar

¼ teaspoon bicarbonate of soda

4 teaspoons of baking powder

200g (8oz) self-raising flour

Before you start
Set your oven at 180°C/350°F/gas mark 4.
You can also bake this pudding in the microwave. Cook it on high for 15 minutes.

For the sauce:

50g (2oz) butter

50g (2oz) dark brown sugar

100g (4oz) golden syrup

Let the pudding cool a little before you eat it as it is very hot.

1.

Mix the sugar, eggs, butter, salt, flour, baking powder and bicarbonate of soda together until it looks like crumbs.

2.

Strain the soaked dates and add. Spoon the mixture into an ovenproof dish and bake for 45 minutes.

3.

Ask an adult for help.

Make the sauce. Put the butter, sugar and syrup into a saucepan. Cook over a low heat until the sugar has dissolved.

4.

Take the pudding out of the oven and pour over the sauce.

Pizza snake

You will need:

- 1 egg
- 1 tablespoon of olive oil
- 2 teaspoons easy blend yeast
- 200g (8oz) plain flour
- 1 teaspoon salt
- black olives
- cheese squares
- 1 teaspoon dried oregano or basil
- green pepper for the snake's tongue
- 5 tablespoons chopped tinned tomatoes (drained of juice)
- 120ml (4fl oz) hot water

Before you start
Set your oven to 190°C/375°F/gas mark 5. Oil a baking sheet.

Mix the flour, salt and yeast in a large bowl.

Mix in the egg, oil and hot water to make a dough.

Knead the dough for five minutes (see page 17).

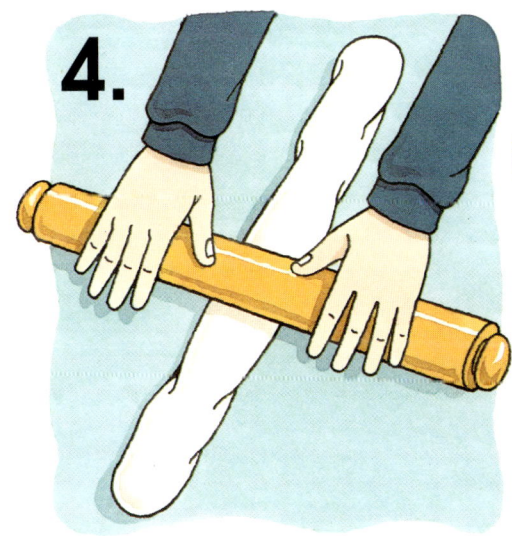

Leave the dough covered in a warm place for an hour. Roll it into a snake.

Curl the snake on a baking sheet. Add tomatoes, herbs and cheese.

Bake for 15 to 20 minutes. Then add the olives and a green pepper tongue.

Popchoc treats

You will need:

25g (1oz) ready-made plain popcorn

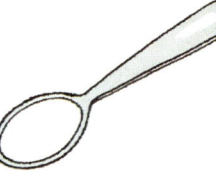
1 tablespoon of water

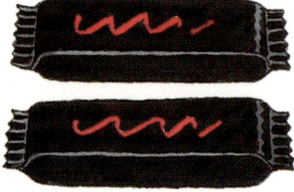
2 chocolate covered caramel bars

75g (3oz) mixed fruit and nuts

1. Chop up the caramel bars. Put them in a saucepan with the water.

2. *Ask an adult for help.*

Put the saucepan over a low heat and stir until the chocolate pieces have melted.

3. Take the saucepan off the heat and stir in the fruit and nuts.

4.

Stir in the popcorn so it is well-coated with chocolate. Let it cool a little.

5.

Form little balls with your hands.

You can leave out the nuts if you don't like them.

Add glacé cherries if you like.

Jam tarts

You will need:

- 200g (8oz) plain flour plus extra flour for rolling
- pinch of salt
- 100g (4oz) margarine or butter
- jam
- pastry cutter
- 1 dessertspoon of sugar
- tartlet tins
- 2 tablespoons iced water

Before you start
Set your oven to 180°C/ 350°F/ gas mark 4. Grease the tins with a little butter.

You can add pastry shapes to your tarts.

Sift the flour and salt into a bowl. Cut the butter into pieces and add.

Rub the butter into the flour until it looks like crumbs.

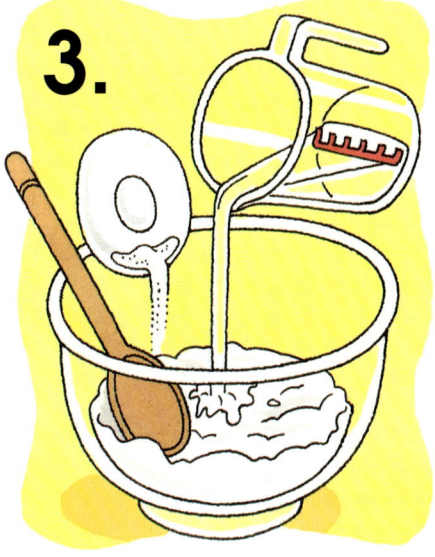

Add the sugar and stir in the water. Mix it into a dough.

Sprinkle some flour onto a surface and roll out the pastry. It should be about 0.5cm (1/4 in) thick.

Cut out rounds of pastry and lay them in the tins. Put a teaspoon of jam into each one.

Bake for about 15 minutes, or until the pastry is golden brown.

Magic marble cake

You will need:

200g (8oz) self-raising flour (sieved)

200g (8oz) butter or margarine

200g (8oz) sugar

1 teaspoon vanilla essence

1 tablespoon cocoa powder (sieved)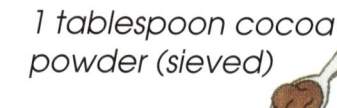

22.5cm (9 inch) cake tin

½ teaspoon pink food colouring*

4 eggs beaten together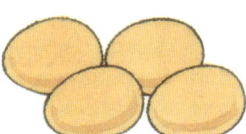

Decorate with choc fudge icing. See page 32 for how to make it.

Before you start
Set your oven to 180°C/350°/gas mark 4. Grease your cake tin with some butter. Then sprinkle in a little flour and shake it. This will stop the cake sticking.

1. Beat the butter and sugar together until fluffy. Stir in the eggs and flour.

2. Divide the mixture into three. Add vanilla to one bowl. Add pink colouring to another and cocoa to the third.

3. Spoon the mixture into the tin, taking turns with each colour. Swirl the colours just once to make a marble pattern.

4. Bake for 40-45 minutes. Leave to cool for a few minutes, then turn it out onto a rack.

* You can buy natural food colours in health food stores.

Choc fudge icing

You will need:

100g (4oz) sugar

120ml (4fl oz) milk

50g (2oz) butter or margarine

150g (6oz) plain chocolate — break it into small pieces.

1. Melt the sugar with the milk over a low heat. Ask a grown-up to help.

2. Bring to the boil, then simmer for two minutes.

3. Take the saucepan off the heat and stir in the chocolate and butter.

4. Cook the mixture for another minute and keep stirring. Leave it to cool and thicken before spreading.